Denali

Denali

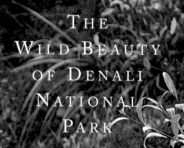

THE WILD BEAUTY OF DENALI NATIONAL PARK

ERWIN AND PEGGY BAUER

SASQUATCH BOOKS
SEATTLE

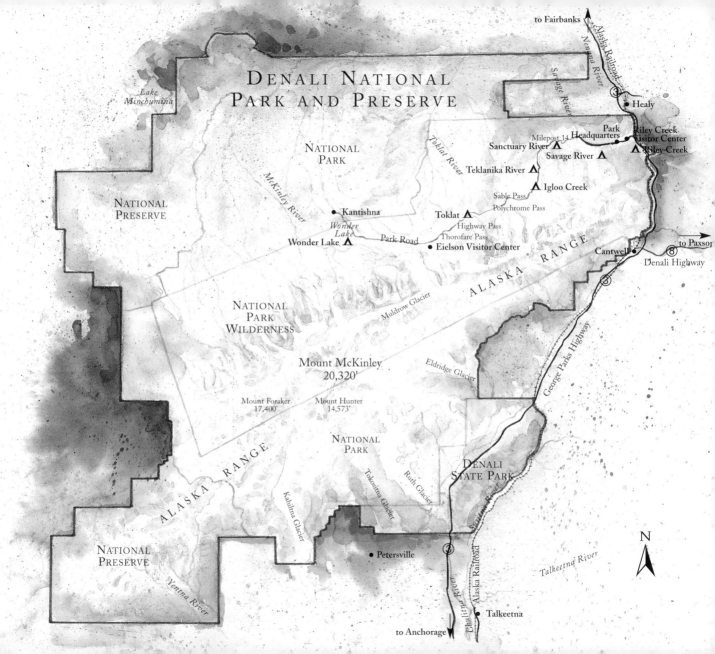

Wolverine below Sable Pass

In the summer of 1906, Charles Sheldon, a wealthy Eastern naturalist and big game hunter, left Fairbanks in interior Alaska on the riverboat the *Dusty Diamond,* and headed downstream on the Tanana River. With him were outfitter-guide Harry Karstens and his five pack horses. Their goal was to study the wild white Dall sheep and other animals

Red fox kits near Savage River den

mostly off the land, they made countless footprints on the mountainsides and in the glacial river valleys of what is known today as Denali National Park and Preserve. One morning, while watching the white crown of the highest peak in North America appear in brilliant sunlight above a gray overcast, Sheldon wrote in his diary that this scenic treasure should be set aside forever as a national park.

Back in New York and Washington, D.C., where the country's political power resided, Sheldon swung into action. Chairman of the influential Game Committee of the Boone and Crockett Club, he convinced the group to endorse a system of game refuges for unspoiled Alaska, particularly for the area he and Karstens had explored. Sheldon buttonholed members of Congress as well as Stephen Mather, director of the fledgling National Park Service (created by Congress in 1916), business tycoons, and builders of the new Alaska Railroad to make this land a people's park on the order of Yellowstone National Park, which had been established in 1872.

In 1917, Sheldon's persistence finally paid off. Both houses of Congress agreed on a bill, which Sheldon personally carried to President Woodrow Wilson to sign, that saved forever the four-million-acre area then known as Mount McKinley National Park. Karstens, who in 1913

that lived just north of the Alaska Range in south-central Alaska. But before the autumn snows curtailed their adventure, the two had wandered over a pristine wilderness paradise few Native Americans and even fewer non-Natives had ever explored. For Sheldon the experience was so powerful that he resolved to spend an entire year in this wonderland.

Sheldon and Karstens returned in the summer of 1907, overwintering well into 1908. Alone and living had made the first ascent of McKinley's south peak, was named park superintendent in 1921. In 1980, under the Alaska National Interest Lands Conservation Act, environmentalist President Jimmy Carter increased the original park area to more than six million acres, and the name was changed to Denali National Park and Preserve. Left unchanged, however, was the name of the great mountain that towered over the park. For obscure reasons, gold prospector William Dickey had, in 1896, named the massive peak after William McKinley, then governor of Ohio and Republican presidential cnadidate, later the twenty-fifth U.S. president. But McKinley never saw the mountain and in fact never even visited Alaska. Today, most Alaskans refer to the mountain simply as Denali, the age-old Athabascan name meaning "the high one."

When measured from the park's lowlands at 2,000 feet above sea level to the summit at 20,320 feet, Mount McKinley's vertical relief of more than 18,000 feet is greater than that of Mount Everest in the Himalayas. Permanent snowfields hundreds of feet deep cover more than 75 percent of the granite core. At only 14,500 feet, a vertical mile below the crest, winter temperatures have plunged to 95 degrees below zero. Storm winds can gust up to 150 miles per hour at any time. The mountain dominates the entire six-hundred-mile arc of the Alaska Range and is considered the heart of the Great Land. Although the peak seems to loom just southwest of the park road at Thorofare Pass, it is really about seventy miles away.

What is so remarkable in this era of human encroachment on wild environments worldwide is that Denali remains largely as pure and unspoiled as Sheldon originally found it. The single, major human-made alteration within the current park boundaries is the park road. Construction began in 1923 and extended westward from park headquarters and the entrance, located on Alaska Route 3 (the George Parks Highway connecting Anchorage and Fairbanks). The Denali Park Road now winds about ninety miles to Wonder Lake and on to Kantishna—once a mining boom town, today almost a ghost village.

The single road makes it possible to pass through absolute wilderness by motor vehicle in one of the world's last undeveloped frontiers. The only other developments within Denali include seven primitive (no electricity) campgrounds, a midpark visitor center (at Eielson), the Denali Park Hotel, simple ranger stations, and a road maintenance complex. Only the first 14.8 miles of the road are paved and accessible to vehicles. This hard-topped section is open from mid-May until autumn snows close it, usually in mid-September. The unpaved portion west of Savage River can be extremely dusty during dry periods, but more often it is sloppy with rain. Only park-authorized shuttle and tour buses are permitted on the unpaved road. Once beyond the road's sights and sounds, a hiker or backpacker can wander over faint

Short-tailed weasel near Riley Creek

game trails throughout the same wilderness that Sheldon explored almost a century ago.

Given enough time, a serious hiker could count hundreds of flowering plants from Denali's lowest elevations to the snowline. And add to these many species of mosses, lichens, and fungi. Only flora that can cope with terribly cold winters and short growing seasons can survive in this subarctic wilderness. Permafrost, ground that has remained frozen for thousands of years, underlies much of Denali, and the topsoil is so thin that the number of plant species here is fewer than elsewhere in Alaska. The river valleys and lower mountain slopes of the park consist primarily of two categories of plant vegetation: tundra and taiga.

Tundra consists of miniature wildflowers and dwarf or stunted shrubs that have adapted to the brief summertime. Moist tundra in Denali is composed of cottongrass and sedge tussocks, dwarf willows, birch, and alder, all rarely taller than knee-high and difficult to traverse. Dry tundra is easy to identify in midsummer by blooming mountain avens, moss campion, dwarf fireweed, saxifrage, and Alaska's state flower, the forget-me-not. Above about 7,000 feet, mosses and lichens replace these leafy plants.

Taiga, a Russian word for northern evergreen forest, describes Denali's riverine lowlands just below the Arctic Circle. Here are quaking aspen, birch, larch, and balsam poplar dominated by black and white spruce, the most common tree species. Mosses and lichens grow on trees and on forest floors, and berries and willows thrive. In the park, taiga exists to about 2,700 feet, or the upper tree limit; above that it is replaced by tundra.

On a cool morning in late June 1955, during the first of many trips to Denali, I had a flat tire on Sable Pass, a halfway point on the park road. At the time only a few hundred of the hardiest car travelers braved central Alaska's "highway" to visit Denali. (Today, the number of visitors annually is nearly 400,000, which has required restricting road access to authorized buses, to avoid congestion and to maintain the wilderness atmosphere.) But my luck turned almost immediately on that day, when the first grizzly bears I had ever seen, a mother with three cubs, appeared nearby. As fast as my trembling hands allowed, I set up a tripod and through an old telephoto lens photographed the grazing, romping animals. Even after a lifetime of filming wild creatures around the globe—from butterflies to Bengal tigers—that first sighting remains an indelible memory.

Hoary marmot at Polychrome Pass, near Riley Creek

The mother bear seemed nervous and eventually she led the family away, running at full speed. Soon I understood why: A large male grizzly, a danger to the cubs, appeared and was attempting to dig ground squirrels from underground dens. I struggled to capture the events on film. In fact, it was dusk before I finally changed my tire and returned to the campground at Igloo Creek. After the male grizzly wandered elsewhere, another female with a nearly full-grown cub came into photographic range, followed by a wolverine. All the while I watched a band of Dall sheep in the distance on the slope of Sable Mountain. No wonder I have returned to Denali time and again, and always after that with my wife, Peggy, who is also a wildlife photographer.

In addition to the unmatched natural beauty of Denali throughout the seasons, and the majesty of the Alaska

Range and Mount McKinley, the beautiful wildlife is most thrilling to visitors. Because no hunting is permitted within the wilderness core of the park and because the wildlife has become accustomed to park buses and human activity, most species may be observed at close range. Denali is the best place in the world, for example, to see gray wolves and grizzlies—both of which are gravely endangered species—living free.

Exploring the winding, often precipitous park road by bus actually improves the wildlife viewing beyond what one can see on one's own. With all of the extra eyes on board to help the experienced driver-guide, not much is missed—from the small arctic ground squirrels to the giant moose bedded in the dense green thickets. The buses pause long enough to allow passengers to watch and photograph anything of interest. Over the years bus riders have witnessed everything from the birth of moose calves to male grizzlies battling for supremacy on a lingering snowfield. The cast of creatures that might be seen on a day trip is extensive, and one sighting that is always sure to cause a stir is that of a gray wolf. Between fifteen and twenty packs, totaling eighty to about a hundred wolves, roam within park boundaries throughout the year. Adult males average about a hundred pounds and females about eighty to eighty-five. The fur color ranges from pure white to solid black, but gray is the predominant color. Wolves are usually spotted hunting smaller animals such as squirrels, marmots, and hares to larger ones such as moose and caribou.

Red foxes have also been seen in the park, abundant in some summers more than others. They are easiest to glimpse in June, when the parent foxes are busy hunting to feed the litters of kits still in dens. Among my most vivid memories of this species is that of a female fox, a thin vixen weighing only about ten pounds, trotting along the gravel road. She was carrying two plump ground squirrels that together must have weighed about four pounds to a den three miles away.

Of Denali's mammals, grizzlies live the longest, in at least one case to twenty years. A one-pound cub born in a deep underground den in January can eventually grow to between five hundred and six hundred pounds. These omnivores depend mostly on grasses, roots, and berries, but grizzlies will eat anything from ground squirrels to the carrion of wolf kills. Because their behavior ranges from savage to curious and playful, grizzly bears inspire more excitement than any other of Denali's wild residents.

Both female and male caribou grow antlers, but those

of the bulls are much larger. The growing antlers have a fuzzy covering, called velvet, which the adult bulls shed in November or December after they have mated. By late summer the bulls, all with enormous, amber-colored racks, gather in small bachelor bands and travel on ancient migration trails that parallel the park road. Cows and young caribou carry their antlers through the winter. Pregnant cows lead the spring migration, heading toward traditional calving grounds mainly south of the Alaska Range. Most caribou spend winter in the taiga, but some winter in the tundra, the northern parts of the park.

Early summer, when snow still covers the high slopes and meadows, is the best time to observe Denali's white Dall sheep. At this time most of the estimated two thousand park animals are nearest the road, although shedding and shaggy in appearance. As always, except during the brief late-autumn breeding season, the rams, with their impressive forward- and outward-curling horns, live in bands separate from the ewes and lambs. The lambs are often born when snow still covers the tundra. Each summer the sheep are seen grazing on avens, grasses, sedges, and willows. Winter survival depends on avoiding wolves and finding enough mosses and lichens beneath the deep snow.

Adult sandhill crane

Moose are the largest of Denali's mammals and, except for caribou, the most abundant. By late August—with velvet dripping from antlers often five feet wide, and gorging on vegetation in a beaver pond near Wonder Lake—a bull might weigh sixteen hundred pounds and measure over seven feet tall at the shoulders. The female the bull will soon find to mate with could weigh more than a half-ton. Moose have provided some of our most exciting moments in the park, from long-limbed mothers nursing calves and giant bulls wading in swollen, silted rivers to a young bull that withstood a wolf's attack for two days before it inevitably died.

Pine marten near park headquarters

Considering the harsh Denali environment and weather conditions, small mammals are fairly numerous; a few species are in fact ubiquitous. Ground squirrels, frequently seen scurrying across the tundra, are the sustenance of many predators, large and small. I have enjoyed sitting near the Eielson Visitor Center in midpark watching ground squirrels' antics, especially when summer's fireweed is in bloom and the sun is shining on "the high one." Motionless, I have also caught glimpses of weasels, martens, lynx, snowshoe hares, red squirrels (especially near campgrounds), beavers (in the ponds near Wonder Lake), voles, and porcupines. Climbing around rock outcroppings, I have spotted collared pikas and hoary marmots.

In addition to these small mammals, a fair number of North American bird species travel vast distances from wintering areas far south to nest in Denali. Wheatears, for example, migrate from Africa. Arctic terns and golden plovers arrive from southern South America. But the easiest bird to see year-round is the willow ptarmigan, the state bird. Families of these birds seem to haunt the roadsides. Some birds, such as the arctic warbler, are far easier to hear than to see.

The darker birds soaring low over the tundra on summer days are short-eared owls or northern harriers searching for voles or lemmings. At higher elevations, especially at spectacular Polychrome Pass, the large brown gliders are golden eagles, which nest annually on the rocky ridges. Such birds of prey as the shy goshawk and the not-so-shy hawk owl hunt in Denali's taiga areas. I have often seen both along the road from the park entrance to the headquarters and just west. Several species of waterfowl nest in Denali—from the common Canada goose to the seldom seen goldeneye and harlequin ducks. By late summer I watch the beaver ponds for other species ready to fly south. A serious birder could count all 163 species that have been recorded at the park. When winter grips the land, however, only the ptarmigans, ravens, gray jays, and black-billed magpies are still around.

In many ways Denali is unique, completely different from other sites in America's splendid national park system. Even in magnificent Yellowstone, the world's first national park, more than a century of human activity has changed the land. In other parks, rivers have been diverted or dammed, natural predators have been eliminated, and other changes to the ecosystem and the environment have been implemented. But Denali's ecosystem remains intact. No long trails have been constructed into the backcountry. With topographic maps in hand, hikers must find their own way or follow game tracks along glacial rivers, over high passes and onto peaks of the Alaska Range. For a closer look at the Dall rams spending summer atop Primrose Ridge, a hiker must switch back on his own path, slowly upward to where the rams graze. In fact, the only maintained trails in the park are the short ones that connect the visitor center to the Denali Park Hotel and to the headquarters. Of course, any backcountry travel can mean the chance of meeting bears.

Another difference between Denali and other parks where grizzlies survive is that no one has ever been killed by a bear in Denali. Long-standing park policy of visitor education and enforcement aimed at keeping apart bears and humans with food has been successful.

Long before Denali became a national park

Collared pika near Eielson Visitor Center

Athabascan Native Americans managed to subsist here year-round—it was not easy. Each winter must have been an ordeal. To hunt and travel, they depended on sled-dog teams, just as rangers use today to patrol the backcountry during winter. Denali maintains the only kennel of active sled dogs in the National Park Service. Among the many daily interpretive services offered by park rangers is a free live demonstration of dog training and a discussion about how dogsledding plays a vital role in park management.

Denali also is different in that it is a favorite destination of the most serious international climbers. Scaling Mount McKinley is dangerous, however, and to date eighty-eight climbers have died in the attempt. Every year, a thousand or so alpinists begin the ascent from Kahiltna Glacier in the Alaska Range—about half are successful. The quest takes about three or four weeks and requires complete dedication and tolerance of foul weather, which hides the peak from park visitors about 65 to 70 percent of the year.

Despite its remoteness and the great travel distance involved, Denali is not a difficult park to visit and enjoy. The easy way is to join one of the many Alaska tours that include or feature Denali. Car travelers will find a variety of lodgings and services in the summer community just north of the park entrance (on Route 3) or at the Denali Park Hotel. Other accommodations geared especially for more active outdoor people are located in and near Kantishna, in the north-central part of the park, at the opposite end of Denali Park Road. In the summer the Alaska Railroad provides daily passenger service from Anchorage and Fairbanks. There is also regularly scheduled bus service.

Summer camping at Denali is so popular that campsites are at a premium. Campgrounds at Riley Creek, Savage River, and Teklanika River are accessible by car or shuttle bus. The Sanctuary River, Igloo Creek, and Wonder Lake sites are only accessible by shuttle bus. Morino campground is reserved for backpackers without transportation (the grounds are located one-quarter mile west of the Alaska Railroad depot).

Arctic ground squirrel at Teklanika Campground

Writing about Denali from a desk far away in Washington State, I am flooded with a cascade of memories about this incomparable wilderness park. I recall the blonde bear we named Frank, known to the busy park rangers simply as "grizzly no. 115." Early in his life, as young male grizzlies often do, Frank got into trouble by trying to eat a sandwich in a hiker's knapsack; the bear later appeared on Anchorage television, when park rangers tranquilized and tagged him.

I also recall how the short Denali summers blend into fall, turning a green landscape into red and gold almost overnight. Sometimes on fall mornings the tundra's glorious color is muted by frost. I remember the caribou bulls, grotesque for a few days as the velvet peels from their antlers, leaving the broad beams a moist, bloody scarlet. Waterfowl fly and beavers stuff their lodges with the season's last green foliage, while paying no attention to the visitors photographing them at close range.

Many of these autumn memories surround the moose, not simply because these are the largest, most impressive deer in the world. One evening, when a weeklong overcast finally lifted and suddenly Mount McKinley was mirrored in the flat calm of Wonder Lake, I witnessed a cow moose and calf standing belly deep in a shallow bay, gorging on succulent aquatic grasses. This scene has symbolized Denali on billboards and brochures for many years, but experiencing it first-hand is different. In the distance a wolf howls and from another direction a second wolf answers. The moment is incredibly stirring.

Another morning, we arrived at Igloo Flats near the heart of the park. Days before, this area of open taiga was empty and silent, except for the jays and white-crowned sparrows. But shortly after daybreak, the place came alive with moose. We counted six females being courted by four bulls of various sizes. Soon two of the largest bulls were squaring off, head to head, grunting and crashing antlers near two busloads of wildlife enthusiasts with cameras in hand. Where else in the world could this happen?

Simply said, Denali is an extraordinary place.

LEFT: *Late in summer, moose are drawn to the succulent vegetation growing in potholes and beaver ponds. They may spend hours browsing in the shoulder-deep water.*

ABOVE: *A cow moose pauses in her underwater browsing to check on her calf nearby. Vulnerable while in deep water, she also watches for wolves.*

RIGHT: *The antlers of this bull are still covered with velvet, but before the breeding season begins in the fall, they will have shed this covering.*

LEFT: *Gray wolves roam and hunt widely throughout Denali National Park, even venturing close to roads, as was this one near Highway Pass.*

RIGHT: *Wide valleys, gravel bars, and braided river courses such as this east fork of the Toklat River have long served as travel routes for wolves, bears, and caribou, as well as for humans.*

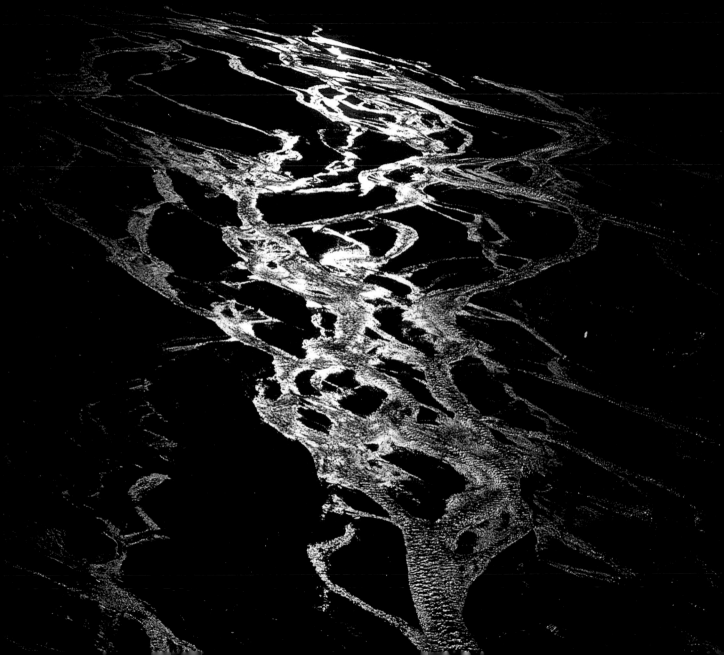

LEFT: *In early autumn the hillsides along the George Parks Highway leading to Denali glow with the golden color of aspens. But the great mountain is hidden beneath ominous skies.*

ABOVE: *Areas where low bush and mountain cranberries (or lingonberries) abound attract grizzly bears, which relish the ripe, bright fruit.*

RIGHT: *The list of wild berries—edible and nonedible—growing in Denali is long. Most colorful in the fall are the bunchberry, or ground dogwood.*

LEFT: *Fed by melting snows from Mount Pendleton, the Toklat River flows northward, illuminated by the late summer sun.*

RIGHT: *The varying, or snowshoe, hare blends into its environment during all seasons. In summer it has a brown coat. By snowfall its fur is white, and thick and warm enough to protect the animal in fifty below zero temperatures.*

BELOW: *In dim, forested park areas, especially along the park's east border, a mycologist can soon find several mushroom species— a few edible, many to be avoided. This is a species of* Pholiota, *edibility uncertain.*

RIGHT: *A change comes over Denali country as summer blends into fall. Suddenly the land, especially the tundra, is a glorious carpet of color. Then all too soon it fades.*

ABOVE: *If any bird can be said to reign over Denali National Park, it is the golden eagle. This is a young one, hatched in a lofty nest near Polychrome Pass and not yet a skillful hunter.*

RIGHT: *A golden eagle scans the open landscape in search of prey. Eagles hunt primarily small mammals, such as marmots and ground squirrels, and larger birds, like the ptarmigan. But they will also pursue the young of larger mammals and will not pass up carrion.*

The lynx of Denali are rarely seen, even fleetingly. But now and then a not-so-shy cat appears, usually around a campground either very early or late in the year. Long legs, a lean body, and large, furry feet enable this furtive cat to stalk and survive winter's deep snow. Lynx depend greatly on a high population of snowshoe hares. When the hare numbers crash—as they do in regular cycles—lynx numbers also fall.

On a bright sunny day, Mount McKinley is a stunning sight. Sadly for many visitors, however, the peak is visible during fewer than half the daylight hours from spring through fall. This view of Denali from near Stony Hill in July is often the first one travelers enjoy.

LEFT: *White, or Dall, sheep are usually visible throughout the park, especially in June when they are below the snow line, feeding on new vegetation.*

RIGHT: *During midsummer, the rams live in bachelor herds, as here on Primrose Ridge, away from the bands of ewes with their lambs.*

LEFT: *The Alaska Range parallels the park road to the south and on bright days glaciated peaks and dramatic vistas are visible for the entire ninety miles.*

BELOW: *The gray, or Canada, jay is conspicuous around campgrounds. It is an alert, opportunistic feeder, caching food for the long winter.*

RIGHT: *White throughout winter and brown in summer, willow ptarmigan live in flocks on shrubby tundra and in alder thickets. This male in transition plumage in late May is singing to declare his territory.*

The journey up Polychrome Pass is a spectacular one. Equally spectacular is the panorama of the Alaska Range to the south. Golden eagles soar here, and herds of caribou or a lone grizzly may wander through the valley below.

FAR LEFT: *Grizzly bears roam everywhere in the park, although only rarely onto glaciers or high peaks. Sable Pass is the best place to find a young one gamboling in summer.*

LEFT: *A near-sighted adult bear stands for a better look at another bear that may be a rival.*

ABOVE: *With a stomach full of green grass and ground squirrels, a grizzly takes time to enjoy July and scratch its back.*

LEFT: *Sleek from a summer of browsing in taiga and tundra, this caribou bull has shed the velvet from its now gleaming antlers.*

RIGHT: *Another caribou bull, still shedding the velvet from its heavy rack, will make its way to the herd's breeding grounds in October, there to duel with other males.*

LEFT: *The red fox is Denali's number one small carnivore. It eats everything from mice and voles to birds' eggs, birds, insects, and berries. This female carries two arctic ground squirrels to hungry kits waiting at an underground den.*

RIGHT: *After kits are fully grown and on their own, an even harder task than raising young is ahead: surviving a seven-month winter.*

LEFT: *West of Polychrome Pass, Dall sheep ewes tend their young where nutritious new grass follows melting snows. The days are long in June and the lambs mature quickly.*

RIGHT: *All activity stops while the Dall mothers scan the landscape for predators.*

LEFT: *Brightly colored and visible along trails to Horseshoe Lake and Riley Creek,* Amanita muscaria *is as poisonous as it is attractive.*

ABOVE: *When viewed close up, Denali's tundra is a tapestry of low-growing plants, green in summer, multicolored in autumn.*

RIGHT: *Alaska's state bird, willow ptarmigan are commonly seen, often feeding on plants. This one is in the rust-brown plumage of summer.*

LEFT: *Watch for hawk owls perched conspicuously in boreal forest openings. They hunt by day for rodents in summer and birds in winter.*

RIGHT: *A shy dweller of forest edges, the merlin is a small falcon that hunts birds and insects by coursing through the sky or dropping suddenly from a perch.*

On a cool, blue, misty morning in September a splendid caribou bull pauses on a ridge overlooking Wonder Lake.

LEFT: *Mount McKinley is so massive and tall that it creates its own weather system. High on the slopes storms develop quickly, and winds can gust to 150 miles per hour.*

RIGHT: *In a forest far below Denali's crest, a young porcupine finds a resting place. In winter, porcupines feed on the inner bark and needles of conifers; in the summer, they eat buds and new plant shoots.*

ABOVE: *Because of the short summer season, beavers in Denali must keep very busy to raise their young, repair dams and lodges, and stock enough food to last the long winter.*

RIGHT: *A young beaver surfaces cautiously before leaving the home pond to cut willow.*

FAR RIGHT: *The area east of Wonder Lake is flooded by dams and an ideal place to watch wild beavers at close range.*

Watch for moose, wolverines, red foxes, and Dall sheep throughout the season at the brooding Sable Pass area.

ABOVE: *Without question Denali National Park is the premier place in the world to observe wild wolves.*

RIGHT: *Depending on the season, wolves hunt alone or in small groups, the latter a necessity for pursuing larger mammals, such as moose and caribou. Hunting is much harder for them when snows are deep and temperatures plunge.*

FAR RIGHT: *Wolves can vary in color from white to black, but grayish coats like these are the most common.*

LEFT: *The shoulder hump and dish-faced profile identify this large male bear as a grizzly rather than a black bear. It is watching a female with a cub on the opposite side of Sanctuary River.*

RIGHT: *Only six months old, this cub is wary and huddles against its mother. In Denali, male grizzlies account for most of the cub mortality.*

LEFT: *The tall lungworts, also called bluebells or chiming bluebells, are among Denali's earliest flowering plants. They bloom in many areas throughout the park.*

RIGHT: *A fine bull caribou walks past Eielson Visitor Center in summer sunshine, with the magnificent Alaska Range as a backdrop.*

Mount McKinley is reflected here in a pond at its closest point to the park road—yet the peak is still 27 miles distant. This vista is considered by many to be the most sublime wilderness scene in North America.

LEFT: *The open taiga landscape east of the park road's Savage River crossing has changed little since Denali was designated a national park.*

RIGHT: *Black bears are widely distributed in Alaska but in Denali are found mainly in the northern and extreme eastern parts of the park, where the terrain is more heavily wooded.*

LEFT: *Among the more exciting birds to see in the park is the gyrfalcon, also known as the arctic falcon, as it flies swiftly over the taiga, hunting other birds.*

ABOVE AND RIGHT: *The pintail drake and red-breasted mergansers share the same beaver pond in the area west of the Eielson Visitor Center.*

LEFT: *During a brief break on a mostly overcast day, Mount McKinley appears just long enough to give visitors a dramatic glimpse of its slopes.*

RIGHT: *Another classic view of Denali National Park is a summer evening on Wonder Lake when a cow moose and calf wade out to browse on aquatic plants.*

ABOVE: *Traveling companions in summer, caribou bulls soon become rivals during the rutting season.*

RIGHT: *On a summer diet of herbaceous plants, grasses, willows, and especially lichens, this bull has grown heavy and symmetrical antlers.*

FAR RIGHT: *Whether this bull is trying to scratch its shoulder, shake off insects, or simply stretch muscles, it takes a strong neck to do it.*

LEFT: *A vital food source for many bird and mammal predators, arctic ground squirrels are extremely important to the park ecology. This one has been gnawing on a discarded moose antler.*

BELOW: *Ripe blueberries are synonymous with summer's end. Wildlife species from willow ptarmigan to grizzly bears relish the fruits, which are more abundant in some years than others.*

The first snow of early fall covers mountains mirrored in Teklanika Pond. Ice fingers form at the pond's edge. Soon everything will be under a still, deep, white blanket.

Published by Sassquatch Books
Printed in Hong Kong
Distributed in Canada by Raincoast Books, Ltd.
04 03 02 01 00   5 4 3 2 1

Cover and interior design: Karen Schober
Map and interior illustrations: Linda Feltner

Cover photograph: A barren ground bull caribou sihouetted in front
of Mount McKinley.
Title page photograph: Pintail ducks.

Library of Congress Cataloging in Publication Data
Bauer, Erwin A.
    Denali: the wild beauty of Denali National Park/photos and text by Erwin
and Peggy Bauer.
      p. cm.
    ISBN 1-570-61209-9
      1. Natural History—Alaska—Denali National Park and Preserve. 2.
Denali National Park and Preserve (Alaska) I. Bauer, Peggy. II. Title.
QH105.A4B38 2000
508.783'3—dc21   00-040083

Sasquatch Books
615 Second Avenue
Seattle, Washington 98104
(206) 467-4300
www.SasquatchBooks.com
books@SasquatchBooks.com

Denali National Park and Preserve
P.O. Box 9
Denali Park, Alaska 99755
(907) 683-2294
(907) 272-7275 or (800) 622-7275 for shuttle, tour bus,
and campground reservations
www.nps.gov/dena/

Established in 1917, the original Mount McKinley National Park was
designated a wilderness area and incorporated into the new 6-million-
acre Denali National Park and Preserve in 1980. In addition to Mount
McKinley—at 20,320 feet, North America's tallest mountain—the
park encompasses breathtaking mountains and glaciers, dynamic
wildlife, and unique taiga and tundra habitats.

The peak season for visiting the park is between Memorial Day and
Labor Day, though the park is open year-round. In summer, the best
way to see the park and spot wildlife is to take a shuttle or tour bus
along the park road. (Note, however, that visitors arriving without
shuttle or tour bus reservations will most likely have to wait one or two
days for an available seat.) Other summer activities include day-hiking,
backcountry camping or mountaineering (permits and registration
required), and attending ranger or naturalist programs. In winter,
cross-country skiing and dog mushing are popular activities, though
extreme conditions can prevail.

Riley Creek Visitor Center, (907) 683-2294, near the entrance to the
park, provides shuttle and tour bus tickets, camping and backcountry
permits, information on accessible day hikes, video programs on such
topics as bear safety, and schedules for ranger-led programs and guided
hikes. There is also a bookstore here, featuring Denali and Alaska
titles, as well as at the Eielson Visitor Center and at the Talkeetna
Ranger Station. Other facilities can be found at the Denali Park Hotel
and in Kantishna.

SELECT BIBLIOGRAPHY

Bauer, Erwin. *Wild Alaska.* New York: Outdoor Life Books, 1988.
Corral, Kimberley, and Hannah Corral and Roy Corral. *My Denali.*
    Seattle: Alaska Northwest Books, 1995.
Elliot, Nan. *Alaska Best Places.* Seattle: Sasquatch Books, 2000.
Murie, Adolph. *Mammals of Denali.* Anchorage: Alaska Natural
    History Association, 1994 (reissue of 1962 edition).
Murie, Adolph. *A Naturalist in Alaska.* Phoenix: University of Arizona
    Press, 1991 (reissue of 1961 edition).
Sherwonit, Bill. *To the Top of Denali: Climbing Adventures on North
    America's Highest Peak.* Seattle: Alaska Northwest Books, 1990.
Washburn, Bradford. *Mount McKinley: The Conquest of Denali.* New
    York: Harry N. Abrams, Inc., 1991.
Waterman, Jonathan. *In the Shadow of Denali: Life and Death on
    Alaska's Mt. McKinley.* New York: The Lyons Press, 1998.

A young red fox

Based on the Olympic Peninsula of Washington State, Erwin and Peggy Bauer
are considered the world's premier wildlife photographers. A prolific husband-and-wife team—
with half a million images in their photo file—the Bauers' photographs have appeared in nature
magazines around the globe and graced more than 300 published covers. Together they have
produced 45 books on wildlife and the outdoors. While the Bauers continue to travel all over the
world to photograph animals and landscapes, they have developed a special relationship with
Alaska in the last 25 years, where they return again and again. They are also the recipients
of many awards, including most recently the prestigious North American Nature
Photography Association's 2000 Lifetime Achievement Award.